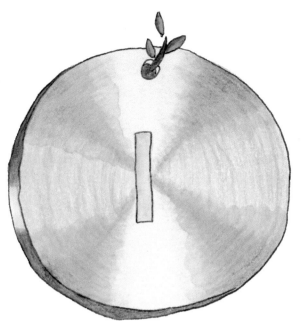

This book belongs to:

. . . .

For T, L, M, A & S

Please leave a review on Amazon

We would love to hear from you

First published in Great Britain in **2020**

Text and illustration copyright @ Kate Yeo, **2020**

Magic Clock Tree and the Monkey Tail Wand

Written and illustrated by Kate Yeo

learn to find the "o'clock" with me

"It feels far too still!" said Miss Hour suddenly.
She jumped up and looked round.
"Now what can it be?"

J ust at that moment,
       the tree where she'd sat
exploded with movement
       and threw her down flat.

The branches were thrashing, the leaves all a jumble, the children alarmed at the deafening rumble.

Before they could get to their feet to escape, a monkey fell out of the tree...

... in a cape!

Untangling himself, he got to his feet,
  and frantically started to search for his treat.
"Found it!" he yelled, picking fruit off the floor.
  Then, looking so sad, said, "I wish I had more."

found it!

"I'm looking for food.
Do you have any here?"

"Yes! You're in luck.
It's our tea time, my dear!"

And with that Miss Hour
laid out snacks on the roots.

"Oh thank you!
I love all these veggies
                    and fruits."

So Monkey joined time school.
He jumped, skipped and hopped,
He swung through the trees.
He just never stopped.

He could not sit still,
not for one little minute.

Where trouble was found
he was sure to be in it.

But...

No sooner had Monkey finished breakfast or lunch
than he was quite ready for more things to munch.

"So what we all need,"
said Miss Hour, "is to show
the **START** of each hour,
so we can all know
exactly when Monkey needs goodies to eat.
We can't have him hungry and down on his feet."

They thought long and hard
and decided to power
the clock with ANOTHER wand
turning each hour.
Miss Hour took the lead,
and it didn't take long
to add to the clock tree a
MONKEY TAIL WAND.

The Magic Clock Tree had the **hour wand** already.
It pointed to **hours**, turning slowly but steady.
Now Monkey's tail wand could be added there too.
So everyone there saw how **fast** the hour flew.

Miss Hour's sparkling wand
was small like a fairy's.
But Monkey's tail wand
was ENORMOUS and hairy.

They painted a picture of veggies and fruit...

...and hung it beside **number 12** on a shoot.
To finish the picture, they added a bell –
a signal that **food o'clock**'s
here now, as well.

T hen...

Miss Hour, on the Monkey Tail Wand, cast a spell.
And slowly it glided away from the bell.
It drifted past all of the numbers in turn,
but took a **whole hour**, much to Monkey's concern.

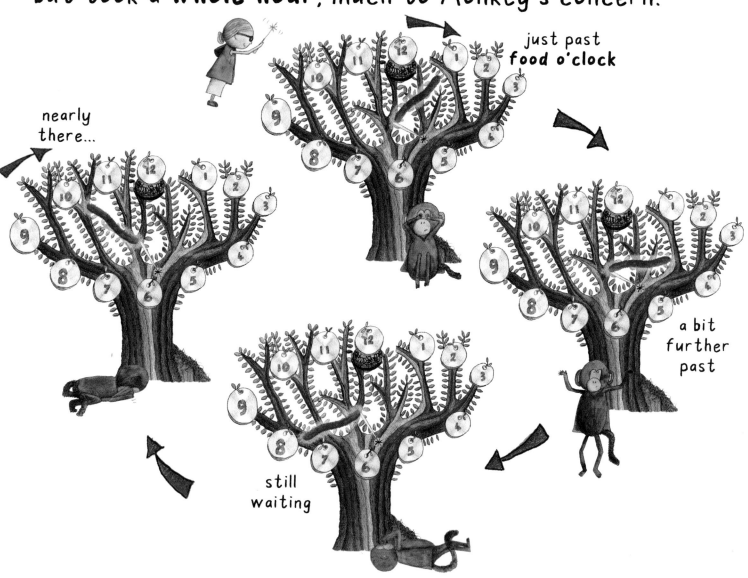

just past
food o'clock

nearly
there...

a bit
further
past

still
waiting

When finally Monkey's tail wand reached the top,
the bell on the **12** dinged: "It's time to stop!"

On hearing the signal, the children decreed:
"It's **food o'clock** Monkey!
Come down from the tree!"

So, Monkey would whizz down and scoop up his snack,
he'd gobble it up and hurry straight back.

But Monkey got greedy and wanted more snacks.
So, waiting until they were turning their backs,
he pushed round the wand 'til it almost reached **12**...

...then ran to the snack log, so pleased with himself.

Their magic provided
his premature treat,
but not quite the snack
he was thinking he'd eat.
"Ha ha!" he giggled
and picked up a pie.
He took a big bite...

...and was pinged to the sky!
He shot up and up like a jet-set harpoon,
unable to stop 'til he got to the moon.

Ho ho!
They had spied him!
They'd tricked HIM instead.
"You can't rush the time silly Monkey!"
they said.
"Now come back to earth! And don't be a cheat!
We'll catch you, dear friend, on this trampoline sheet."

So Monkey jumped back down to earth, to the wood.
The children had helped him, as all good friends should.
And from that day on, he waited his turn.
The snacks can't be hurried, that's one thing he'd learn!

Now you! Can you search out the **12** on your clock? When **Monkey's tail wand**'s there, it's their 'snack **o'clock**!'

Your next job's to look for **Miss Hour's tiny wand**. It shows the **hour number** it's centred upon.

Take note of the **number** Miss Hour's wand points out.
You'll need it to tell which **o'clock**'s come about.

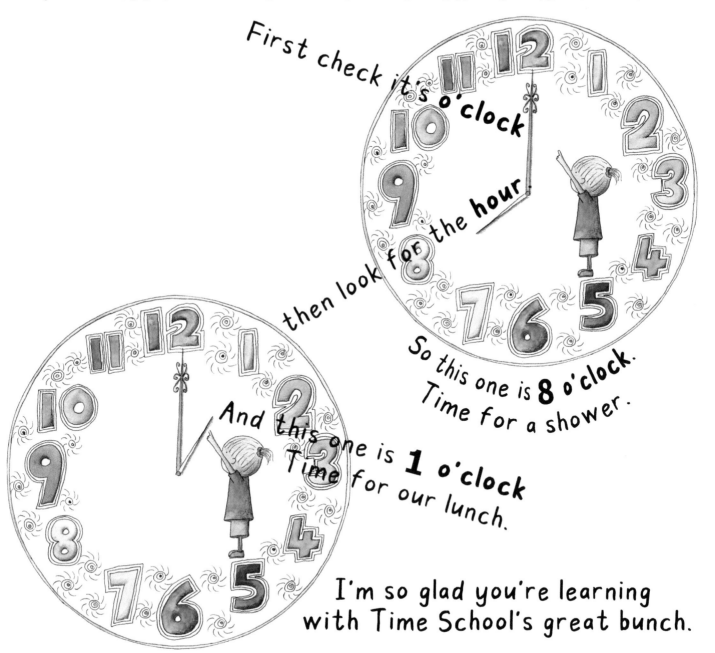

First check it's **o'clock**

then look for the **hour**.

So this one is **8 o'clock**.
Time for a shower.

And this one is **1 o'clock**
Time for our lunch.

I'm so glad you're learning
with Time School's great bunch.

Now practice, and read, and play with it more,
as telling the time takes some learning, for sure.

P.S.

Outside the magical world of time school,
the '**Hour Wand**'s' called '**Hour Hand**' and that's pretty cool.

The '**Monkey Tail Wand**'s' often named '**Minute Hand**',
but they don't know Time School, so can't understand!

Plus, we think it's fun learning time with Miss Hour
and Monkey, to show us **o'clock**'s super power!

Make an o'clock spot

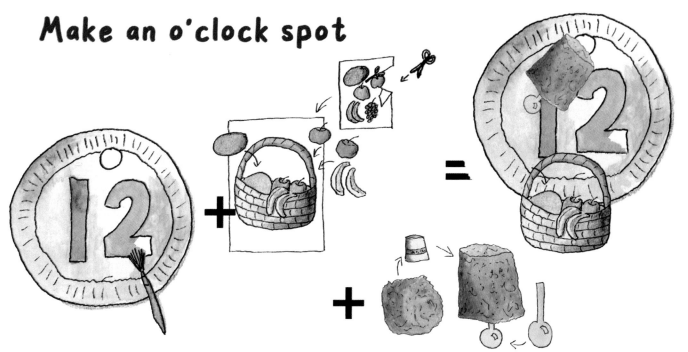

Let's Play

Show which way the wands turn

Be a long monkey tail wand ... or a small hour wand

Make a long monkey tail wand

Make a small hour wand

Playing is learning

Paint a picture

Make a magic clock tree

I hope you enjoyed reading
The Magic Clock Tree and the Monkey Tail Wand.
Learning to read the time is notoriously tricky for many children.

Traditionally, all the elements of telling the time are often introduced all at once (hour, minute, long and short clock hands, quarter and half, past and to).

This series of books addresses each element gently and gradually. The characters and storylines explain why things are as they are — according to Miss Hour!

Don't forget to 'play' the book. See the Let's Play pages for ideas. Children love to play freely with a few props, get messy, make mistakes (very important to feel safe to do that!)
That's when their learning is the most natural, arguably the most effective, and certainly the most fun!

The Magic Clock Tree and The Monkey Tail Wand
is the second book in the series.
Watch out for the next ones.

I'm a mum of four young children and a Speech and Language Therapist. Writing and illustrating are completely irresistible to me and keep me energised!
I am often to be found "between sleeps" in the small hours indulging in my latest project.

Printed in Great Britain
by Amazon

82304724R00020